THEY DIED TOO YOUNG

SID VICIOUS

BY
Tom Stockdale

This edition first published by Parragon Books Ltd in 1995

Produced by
Magpie Books Ltd, London

Copyright © Parragon Books Ltd 1995
Unit 13–17, Avonbridge Trading Estate, Atlantic Road
Avonmouth, Bristol, BS11 9QD

Illustrations courtesy of: Rex Features: Associated Press

ISBN 0 75250 689 7

A copy of the British Library Cataloguing in Publication
Data is available from the British Library.

Typeset by Hewer Text Composition Services, Edinburgh
Printed in Singapore by Printlink International Co.

'My basic nature is going to kill me in six months'. This was a comment from Sid Vicious during a telephone call with photographer Roberta Bayley, while he was in hospital in New York in January 1978. Sid was admitted to the Jamaica Hospital after a heroin overdose which everyone around him had been expecting since he had started to play out the part he felt was expected of a rock star. The tragedy of the life and death of Sid Vicious is one of an impressionable youth, who rose to prominence with the Sex Pistols, arguably the most influencial band since the revolution of the Beatles in the 1960s.

It has been said that the music of the 1970s can be split into pre- and post-Pistols and their glorious negativity. As the midwives of Punk Rock in 1975, they mirrored a disaffection amongst the young in a Britain which was diving into economic depression and unemployment, and espoused a creed which rejected most of the rock and pop music which was around them. Johnny Rotten was generally acknowledged as the king of Punk Rock, but Sid Vicious was the myth made man; in a movement known for the importance of attitude over ability, Sid made himself into the object that the world feared would rise from Punk, without thinking where it might lead him. It led to a frozen point in time which put him, at the age of twenty-one, into the gallery of rock rebels, and it is doubtful, if he had been offered the choice, whether he would have taken another option. As Dick Hebdige noted at the time Sid had 'done it his way'.

How to Manufacture
Your Group

Sid Vicious was born John Simon
Ritchie on 10 May 1957 in London
and raised mostly in London. His
mother, Ann Beverley, had had a hard
childhood, being abandoned by her
unmarried mother when she was
twelve, marrying young, and having
Sid by another man, John Ritchie, with
whom she lived for two years on Ibiza.
On their return to London, Ann and

young John took the treatment that was meted out to one-parent families – they moved too many times to count, and John went to as many schools. She used to call him Simon Ritchie, though to childhood friends he was John Beverley (Beverley being Ann's second husband's name). Ann was a firm member of the hippy movement while John was a child and took him on the hippy trail when he was ten. She was no stranger to drugs, and in 1979 would be detained with two other people by the police after 25lbs of cannabis was found in a Paddington flat. John's upbringing gave him an early awareness of the hardship and violence of his local neighbourhood, and although he was not a fighter he was able to take care of himself, and had learned a healthy disrespect for authority, although he and his mother were close. He left school at 15 and worked in a clothing factory, before going to college for a photography course.

It was in 1973 at Hackney Technical College that John Beverley met John Lydon, a long-haired, fiercely independent Londoner of Irish parents, and just over a year older than Beverley. Beverley was a happy opposite to Lydon's cynical personality, and was already making himself noticed as a follower of the glam style which Marc Bolan and David Bowie were bringing to prominence. Beverley would wear sandals without socks to show off his varnished toe-nails, even during the winter; he would go out without a coat if he wanted to show off a new shirt, and he followed Bolan into the world of the permanent wave. He had a great deal of trouble getting his hair to stand up like Bowie's did, and tried hanging his head upside-down in the oven in an attempt to achieve success.

Together with Lydon, an old friend of his, John Gray and another John, John Wardle (later Jah Wobble), Beverley learned to drink. For Lydon it was an escape from his work, firstly on a sewage farm and then at a shoe shop. Lydon renamed Beverley Sid after his pet hamster, which was also called Vicious after it had bitten Lydon's father, and the two names stuck for the tall, non-violent looking Beverley.

Ann Beverley had made her son leave home, so Sid started a period of squatting in empty flats, and when Lydon was given his marching orders from his parents' house after hacking off his hair and a dyeing clash with his yellow hair which turned it bright green, they lived together, ending up in the wealthy area of Hampstead. They enroled for A-levels, but rarely attended classes, although Lydon enjoyed some of the English Literature course. They worked for a time at Cranks health food restaurant on the Tottenham Court Road. Sid started to sell speed which gave him all the money he needed to live; speed, along with alcohol, would become the drug of the Punk movement. John Gray recalled Sid injecting a mixture of speed and amphetamine sulphate, asking where he got it from, and receiving the reply, 'it's me mum's'. Lydon got a job at a children's play centre during school holidays, but his appearance brought complaints from worried parents. Lydon gave Sid a DIY haircut, and the pair started to burn themselves with cigarettes, simply out of curiosity. When the press later picked up on this habit after he had stubbed out cigarettes on the back of his hand during a gig, Lydon retorted 'pain doesn't hurt. I do it for my own amusement'.

The two would go busking down on the underground, singing the same Alice Cooper song again and again, and started going to gay clubs, where they found freedom from the harassment that they started to encounter at other clubs. They would dance like dervishes to the current disco hits, creating a surreal impression and a lot of space on the dance floor. Sid was still heavily into David Bowie, and would go to see him whenever he could. The group that they gathered around them had all the attitude anyone could ask for, all that was needed was a channel to direct themselves down, and they found that in a group of people based around Malcolm McLaren.

McLaren, born on 22 January 1946, grew up with the fashion business, as his father owned a clothing factory in London. He was badly behaved at school, but found that college life suited him. Starting with a course at St Martin's School of Art in 1963, he proceeded on a six-year trail around the art schools of London gathering influences from various art and style sources, and soaking up the political freedoms of the student liberals. In 1965 he met Vivienne Westwood, five years older than him, and running away from a failed marriage. She was an artistically inclined teacher, who moved in with McLaren, and they had a son in 1967.

Westwood was a practical aid to McLaren's creative urges, and in 1971 they moved into a shop at 430 King's Road, selling 50s memorabilia under the name Let It Rock. They received favourable press coverage and the shop became known as a place where people could hang out, as well as buy goods from the rock'n'roll era of McLaren's rebel heroes like Billy Fury, Gene Vincent and Eddie Cochran. By 1973

Sid Vicious

The young Sid was heavily into
David Bowie

McLaren had renamed the shop Too Fast To Live, Too Young To Die and Westwood was making changes to the clothes they bought for the Teds who were their main customers. The chance to sell in New York was leapt upon by McLaren, and there he met members of the band New York Dolls, the cross-dressing, high-energy, Warhol-influenced rockers. The band excited his instincts for style and music and their combined ability to shock.

McLaren returned to London determined to bring the shop into the present, and a major refit resulted in the new name, Sex. McLaren and Westwood started to buy in and make rubber and leather clothes based around the usually back-alley world of the sex shop.

They also put political slogans onto shirts and T-shirts, which started to sell well to the bored teenagers who had started to hang out on the Kings Road.

One early fan of the relaxed atmosphere at McLaren's shop was Steve Jones, a classic product of a broken home and a committed juvenile criminal, with fourteen convictions for various offenses. He and an old friend, Paul Cook, had formed a band in 1972 with another mate, Wally Nightingale. Jones' criminal activities supplied them with quality instruments and amplifiers. Their most high profile break-in was to the Hammersmith Odeon before a David Bowie concert in July 1973, which yielded sixteen guitars and a complete PA with all its microphones. They called themselves the Strand, after the Roxy Music song, and were influenced by the Small Faces, the Kinks, the Stooges and the New York Dolls.

Jones used to harass McLaren about the band, until, at the end of 1973, McLaren found them some rehearsal space and put his mind to the possibilities contained in a group of awkward aggressive lads who wanted to make a lot of noise. A note of musical ability was injected into the band at this time with the addition of seventeen-year-old Glen Matlock, who was working in the shop, on bass. Paul Cook, the same age as Matlock, was the drummer, eighteen-year-old Jones took the vocals, and Nightingale was on guitar.

The Sex Pistols

Amongst the people gravitating to the Kings Road were the 'four Johns'. They came out of boredom, and used to abuse the fashion shoppers of the area, 'gobbing at the posers and pissing around', as Lydon described it. Their clothes came mostly from jumble sales and their hair looked infectious; Lydon's green, Gray's lilac and Sid's so full of vaseline that to lend him a pillow was to have it basted. Their image cut right through the prevailing style, which was still that of the long hair and flared trousers which accompanied chart hits of early 1974 such as 'You won't find another fool like me' by the New Seekers and Paper Lace's 'Billy don't be a hero'. They saved most of their scorn, however, for the top groups such as Yes and Pink Floyd, whose large-scale concerts gave fans no point of contact with the stars. It seemed that the rebellion which rock had begun in the 1960s had petered out in a record company-controlled commercialism which packaged the dream into something acceptable to the older generation, but boring to the new youth.

Throughout 1974 the Strand continued rehearsing, and when McLaren left for New York in November he had already formulated the idea for a band which would be a promotional tool for the shop. Thus the celebrated Sex T-shirt 'You're going to wake up one morning and *know* what side of the bed you've been lying on' listed, on the 'loves' half of a 'loves/hates' catalogue, 'Kutie Jones and his SEX PISTOLS'. McLaren's trip to America was to manage the New York Dolls, who were on the point of breaking up. For six months McLaren attempted to relaunch the band, clothing them in Westwood-designed red, with attendant hammer and sickle backdrop and the slogan 'what are the politics of boredom? Better red than dead'. However, the Dolls' time was up, and they had been superseded by a new line of naturally angry musicians like Television, Patti Smith and the Flamin' Groovies.

McLaren returned to London when the New York Dolls finally split up, in the spring of 1975, with some valuable management experience and ideas for a singer based on his impressions of Television's vocalist, Richard Hell, whom he had asked to come to Britain to front a new band. McLaren put his ideas to work on the Strand, getting rid of Wally Nightingale and putting Steve Jones on guitar. The search for a singer brought offers to several young street-wise youths, among them Midge Ure, who was too busy with his band Slik.

It was in August 1975 when Bernie Rhodes, friend of Malcolm McLaren and soon-to-be manager of the Clash, saw John Lydon in his 'I hate Pink Floyd' T-shirt, and invited him to

Sex. It was instantly obvious to McLaren that here was someone with the front to lead a band, and the audition – an over-the-top rendition of Alice Cooper's 'Eighteen', got him the job. Jones, Cook and Matlock took an instant dislike to his aggressive manner, but McLaren insisted. What McLaren could not have guessed was the way in which his plans for an outrageous way to advertise his shop would become the monster that Lydon's aggression and charisma fed on. McLaren thought he was aiming for pop revolution; what he got was a musical terrorist force, which would uncover a seam of discontentment, and refuse to be broken by the storm of fear and hatred that rose against them. And around the band there

Punk fashion

Malcolm McLaren

gathered a coven of hard core fans, led from the very first by Sid Vicious.

Lydon's influence on the band was immediate. He took on the lyric-writing duties, and this would be just one of the causes of conflict between him and Glen Matlock, who had more of a melodic nature and didn't agree with the virulence of the words which Lydon wrote. By November 1975 the band was ready for their first gig at St Martins School of Art, and John Lydon had his new name, chosen by Steve Jones for the state of Lydon's teeth; Johnny Rotten. The name Sex Pistols was chosen only just before the gig. They played five songs before the power was cut off, but Adam Ant, a member of the main band Bazooka Joe, was impressed by their tightness, their presence and their expensive equipment! 'I left Bazooka Joe the next day' he says.

It was soon apparent that booking concerts would be a problem, and they succeeded for a while by simply arriving at venues and saying that they had been told they could play. Money, of course, was tight, and Chrissie Hynde, a streetwise American friend who would soon present herself to the world as the singer of the Pretenders, got Sid and Johnny cleaning jobs. She also managed to get Sid some modelling work at St Martins. He spent some time selling at Sex (although he was found out slipping a rubber T-shirt to a friend). The T-shirts cost more than money to wear; Rotten was taken to hospital after wearing one for a gig, and Vicious collapsed in the same garment after walking around in the summer heat.

Paid employment took second place as the Sex Pistols set about nine months' gigging up and down the country, gathering small numbers of converts at each venue, and encouraging the growth of other groups with the attitude of 'just get up there and do it'. Bands like Souxsie and the Banshees, the Buzzcocks and Penetration were formed as a direct response to seeing the Pistols. Other bands like the Damned and the Clash got together from the group in London around Malcolm McLaren. It was often hard to play a venue more than once; the aggressive performances meant that equipment got damaged, and the atmosphere spread from the Pistols to the crowd. They gained a reputation for bringing violence with them, starting with a fight which Vivienne Westwood instigated, and which Sid threw himself into, at a Nashville Club gig in April. A ban was the result. The quote from Steve Jones that 'we're not into music, we're into chaos' brought the beginnings of newspaper attention that would grow into a feedback loop of media hunger for Sex Pistols headlines.

The Pistols managed to get a series of weekly gigs at London's 100 Club, and it was at one of these that Sid is credited with having invented the Pogo dance. Although created possibly from the need simply to see the band, it caught on with the regular crowd and became a vital response to any concert by any of the bands now gathering under the name of 'Punk', a term of abuse borrowed from the cop shows and garage bands of 60s America.

In April 1976 the influential first album by the Ramones hit Britain. Sid was an immediate fan, and his later bass technique would owe much to Tommy Ramone's example. As the Pistol's number one fan he took the violent image to heart. He started to carry a bicycle chain and would clear a whole dance floor by swinging it. He narrowly escaped being arrested for carrying it in the street, and was responsible for an attack with a chain on journalist Nick Kent at a 100 Club gig on 3 July. Film director Julian Temple, who got his first filming experience with the Sex Pistols, remembered a Clash concert where Sid dived out from behind the stage onto a group of glass-throwing heavy metal fans, not caring what happened to him after he landed in amongst them. He was arrested in September 1976 during the 'Punk festival' which McLaren set up to gain media coverage for the Pistols, after throwing a glass towards the Damned, who were on stage. It hit a pillar and splintered over the crowd, wounding a girl in the eye. Sid got beaten up and was taken to Ashford remand centre; the institution gave him nightmares, but it resolved him in his belief in total personal freedom. He was given food for thought in the Charles Manson book that Westwood lent him to read. Sid's court appearance

The early Sex Pistols line-up in Amsterdam

The Damned

for the offence in December prevented him fulfilling an agreement with Chrissie Hynde to marry her so that she could stay in Britain; he had offered to do it for £2, and when she had dragged him down to a registry office the day before it had been closed for a holiday.

By this time the Sex Pistols had developed a regular set which included over half of the twenty-five or so songs that the band recorded before they split up. Numbers included the Stooges' 'No Fun', 'New York', 'Satellite', 'Submission', 'Liar' and the song that would become the first Punk anthem, 'Anarchy in the UK'. They were also doing a good job of advertising the clothes from Sex which they would wear onstage. The clothes were not cheap, but the T-shirts especially were very popular with those who wanted to show their solidarity with the growing Punk movement as well as shocking their elders. Soon, McLaren and Westwood would come up with the bondage trousers – made with strapping between the legs – which became one of the most memorable images of the time. The hair remained hacked rather than cut, and the mohican style still celebrated on picture postcards from London would not become popular until after the film *Taxi Driver* in 1978. The predominant dress was one which mixed various styles, from the Teddy Boy jackets and shoes, to black leather and jumble-sale knitwear.

The most accessible accessory was the safety pin; worn in the lapel, on the body or used to attach sleeves onto jackets, it was the cheapest instant way to be recognised as a follower on the streets. John Lydon was given a dress suit by his parents, took it upstairs, and appeared a short time after with it torn apart and pieced together with safety pins – from traditional drab to cutting edge in several easy moves. The other end of the extreme was the use of the swastika, an emblem which gave a deal of hurt to many people. It was used by punks as the taboo which it was considered could not be broken, rather than as any fascist alignment. As the mid-70s saw the growth of the National Front in Britain it gave the punks the label of fascist sympathizers which they did not, on the whole, agree with.

Sid Vicious is best known from photographs of him wearing the black leather jacket that made any street youth suddenly look dangerous. He would accessorize with garters outside his jeans, or a padlock over his crutch. He wore a lot of clothes from Sex, and was encouraged in his outlandishness by McLaren, who saw him as a figurehead for his revolt against the norms of society. Together with his aping of Johnny Rotten (who had a much more realistic idea of the theatricality he was involved in), Sid became more and more the very image of Punk, ready to change his mind about something at a moment's notice, especially if he could wind someone up by doing so.

He was determined to be in a band himself. He taught himself the rudiments of the bass guitar in one night, with the help of the Ramones album and a supply of speed. He was the singer in a band called the Flowers of Romance by Rotten, after an early Pistols song, which rehearsed but never played, and which contained a variety of other members, some of whom never even considered themselves to be in the band. At the 'Punk festival' in September he was the drummer for Siouxsie and the Banshees' first gig at the 100 Club, and he attempted to move on to the saxophone; as he said, in a comment about learning to play an instrument, 'you just pick a chord, go twang and you've got music'. He wrote some lyrics, with titles such as 'Piece of Garbage', 'Brains on Vacation' and the particularly offensive 'Belsen was a Gas'.

How to Sell the Swindle

While Sid Vicious was honing his Punk
persona, the Sex Pistols were being led
by Malcolm McLaren towards a record
deal. He touted a demo tape made in
July 1976 around the major companies,
as he was determined to strike a deal
with someone who could come up with
a good financial offer, as well as provid-
ing the distribution that the independent
companies could not give. These small
companies, such as Chiswick and Stiff,

had started to spring up as a response to the 'this is a chord, now form a band' creed which the fanzine *Sideburns* put so succinctly. The Pistols had received their first airing on national television, playing 'Anarchy in the UK' on the *So It Goes* programme, but by the beginning of October there was only EMI or Polydor who were interested in taking a chance on the band.

EMI were the first to make the jump, offering a £40,000 advance, in a two-year contract which was drawn up in a single day. The deal was signed on 8 October 1976, and McLaren had got a band which almost no one in the industry liked a very respectable agreement. The Sex Pistols also signed a management contract with Glitterbest, a company that McLaren had bought 'off the shelf'. They gave 25% of their earnings to Glitterbest over three years, with 50% of the merchandising, and McLaren was deemed to own the rights to the Sex Pistols' name. They were not given a chance for independent advice, and in any case weren't bothered about the possible repercussions from a disadvantageous agreement in the future. It would take eight years after the break-up of the band to sort the mess out, and the lawyers ended up with most of the money.

The Sex Pistols had seemingly pulled some very expensive wool over the eyes of a major record company, and the tabloids latched onto a mixture of truth and myth which would confuse many of those inside the movement, as well as most of those outside it. The Clash and the Damned were making moves on the position of the Pistols as the premier Punk band and a single was needed in a hurry to capitalize on the high-profile recording contract. The single was 'Anarchy in the UK', but it was beaten into second place for first Punk single by the Damned's 'New Rose'.

The producer for 'Anarchy' was Chris Thomas, who had made his name with the bands the Pistols hated, the Beatles and Pink Floyd, but the treatment he gave the song made it an impressive debut, with Lydon's sneering tone cutting through a wall of guitar. Its anti-nationalist sentiments and ripped up Union Jack advertisement were a considered statement to the population.

Shortly after the release of the single on 26 November, another EMI group, Queen, dropped out of a planned interview on the *Today* programme, hosted by Bill Grundy. The Pistols and a group of fans were brought to the television studios at only two hours' notice on 1 December. They took advantage of the alcohol in the hospitality room and were goaded by Grundy into a series of four-letter words which jammed the phone lines to the studios and brought banner headlines in the press for the next three days. From then on the Sex Pistols were the main act in a media circus. They would be invited to provide violent or shocking headlines: in Leeds a journalist offered £20 for the sight of some potted plants being kicked around, and even the clearing of a throat could be

Siouxsie and the Banshees

The Sex Pistols on stage

interpreted as an act of aggression for the morning editions.

The uproar that resulted from the Grundy episode meant that the Pistols' tour, due to begin three days later, was hit by cancellations and town council bans. Only three of the planned nineteen dates were played and an estimated £10,000 was lost as a result, although 'Anarchy in the UK' was in the top thirty at number 27. With the impossibility of playing in the UK, the band took a short promotional tour of Holland, gaining 'Rotten sick at Heathrow' headlines. It was the final straw for EMI, who had been taking a lot of internal flak for their association with such a monstrous creation. The Sex Pistols were dropped from the label while they were in Holland, although they fell with the recording advance and publishing money in their hands.

The last Dutch gig was also Glen Matlock's final show with the band. The antagonism between him and Johnny Rotten got too much for him, and when Sid started to turn up for rehearsals Glen decided not to fight. He went on to form the Rich Kids, and would continue to collect royalties on two-thirds of *Never Mind The Bollocks*, a clear indication of how missed his songwriting would be. However, Sid was now in the band, and would start to live the life he considered vital to someone of his rock status.

In the *Sounds* readers' Poll at the end of 1976, The Sex Pistols were voted tenth best new band, with 'Anarchy in the UK' eighth best single, as well as number one worst single. In the *NME* Poll, Johnny Rotten was voted top of the Most Wonderful Human Being category.

Before Sid could show himself on stage in his new role, there was the matter of a new record company to sort out. The Sex Pistols signed to A&M Records on 9 March 1977 for £75,000, with a symbolic signing outside Buckingham Palace the day after. At the following press conference the Pistols went straight for the alcohol, and Sid swigged from a vodka bottle through the entire conference. They took more bottles back to

the limousine, and started a fight on the
way to the A&M office, during which
Sid lost his shoes and cut his foot. He
collapsed in the office with a daffodil in
his lap, and was woken up with some
wine thrown in his face. Rushing into
the toilets to deal with his injury he
broke a toilet, put his elbow through a
window and bathed his foot in another
toilet bowl. The band was gathered
together to return to their rehearsal
rooms on Denmark Street, though they
had to take mini cabs, since the limousine driver refused to have them back in
the car. Sid collapsed onto a bed, saying
'this is my first day and as far as I'm
concerned it's great being in the Sex
Pistols'. Then he passed out. Later that
day Rotten was fined for possession of
amphetamine sulphate, and then he and

Johnny Rotten

Poster for 'God Save the Queen'

Sid went to the Speakeasy club and had a
fight with Bob Harris, presenter of *The
Old Grey Whistle Test* and good friend of
Derek Green, A&M's A&R man.

Realising just what he had let his company in for, Green contacted Jerry Moss,
the boss in America, and on 16 March, a
week after signing, A&M and the Sex
Pistols parted company. The Pistols had
taken a total of £125,000 from the two
record companies and McLaren com-
mented, 'I just keep going in and out of
doors and people keep giving me che-
ques'. The split also caused the destruc-
tion of 25,000 copies of 'God Save the
Queen' which had been pressed ready
for release.

How To Become
The World's No.1 Terrorist
Attraction

Sid's joining of the Sex Pistols occurred
at the same time as the beginning of the
other great involvement of his life, his
meeting with Nancy Spungen, who at
nineteen was a year younger than Sid.
Nancy had been undergoing therapy
since a hyperactive childhood in Phila-
delphia, had twice tried to commit
suicide and had run away to New York

from college. She had become infamous on the American rock circuit as a groupie and heroin addict, and came over to London with Johnny Thunders, who had been in the New York Dolls and who had brought his new band, the Heartbreakers, to test the British waters. It is Thunders who is said to have brought heroin into the British punk scene, and Nancy who brought it to Sid Vicious.

Nancy was almost universally disliked, not least by Johnny Rotten, who blamed himself for pushing her onto Sid after rejecting her overtures. Rotten described her as 'the Titanic looking for an iceberg'. Sid's character was no match for Nancy's sex and drugs combination, and their getting together meant that he

and Rotten lost the close friendship that
they had had. Sid had claimed that he
was 'one of the most sexless monsters
ever' and that people were 'very un-
sexy', but Nancy was the love of his life
and the two were soon to become
inseparable. She helped to persuade
him that he was the star of the Sex
Pistols and he soon started to act like
it, losing any of the more normal social
urges that he once possessed.

To get back into the swing after the
media shows of the record deals, McLaren managed to get a gig at the Notre
Dame Hall, which was quite a coup,
with the new negative publicity on top
of the venue bans already in effect. The
gig was filmed for an American television show and only 150 fans were

allowed to participate. It was Sid Vicious' first public performance, and he showed all the aggression that would now associate itself formally with the Pistols. They left for a break in Jersey the next day, but were given twenty-four hours to leave the island and went on to Berlin. Here they spent their time getting into scrapes with film crews, and couldn't go into East Berlin because Sid had not brought a passport.

While the Pistols were away, McLaren managed to arrange a gig at the Screen on the Green in Islington, London, for 3 April. Entrance was free and the show included a screening of a film about the Pistols, 'Sex Pistols Number One'. Three days later, Sid was in hospital with hepatitis. He was out of action

44

for a month, during which McLaren worked hard for another record deal. Nancy was one of the few people who visited him in hospital, and this period sealed their relationship.

Other bands were doing deals and bringing out records and the Pistols were in danger of losing any commercial advantage. The Damned's *Damned Damned Damned* had been first to hit the streets, and the Clash's eponymous first album was released before a nationwide tour in May 1977 which put their more positive rebellion firmly on the map. Another string of groups like the Stranglers and the Jam were starting to get deals in a more approachable rock format which would become the New Wave follow-up to Punk.

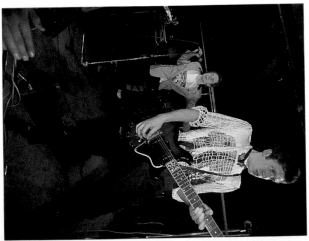

Sid Vicious joined the Sex Pistols in 1977

A fan supports the band's message

The rescue for the Sex Pistols came in the shape of Richard Branson's Virgin Records company. Branson had the advantage of being able to make decisions on his own for his company, and wanted a way out of the backwater that the slowdown in sales of the phenomenal *Tubular Bells* had left him in. McLaren did not like Branson's hippy image, and they both had imaginative business methods that made them a challenge to each other, but they needed each other too, so on 12 May a £50,000 advance was agreed and signed (Sid signed three days later when he was allowed out of hospital). There was now a rush on to get 'God save the Queen' released in time for the prime marketing period of the Silver Jubilee week of 9 June.

Despite a down-tools by the pressing plant, whose workers protested against the material in the song, it was on sale from 27 May, and went into the charts at number 11, although television and radio stations refused to advertise it (though of course John Peel played it), and Woolworths, Boots and W H Smith refused to stock it. The song had everything; timing, notoriety and attitude, around a roaring, joyous hymn against all the nationalism that the Jubilee presented. The Sex Pistols had put their music where their mouths were, and had declared themselves against the state.

As publicity for the Jubilee itself, McLaren booked a boat on the Thames, called the *Queen Elizabeth*, for a party at which the Sex Pistols played. As they approached the Houses of Parliament they launched into 'Anarchy in the UK'. A scuffle in the crowd gave the nervous captain his excuse to radio for the police, and the *Queen Elizabeth* was manoeuvred to Charing Cross Pier. After a stand-off between fans and police the party disembarked, while the Pistols slipped off from a hidden stairwell. There was a glaring lack of reporting of the incident, and 'God Save the Queen' only got to number 2 in the charts that week, despite selling a lot more records than the number 1, Rod Stewart's 'I Don't Want to Talk About It'. Apparently the chart return shops were changed for that week to disallow the Virgin record shops, where a good proportion of the single's sales were made.

The following week, the press resumed its Pistol-packed headlines, and the country as a whole poured a stream of hatred down onto the band. The Punks were seen as a symbol of the increasing hardships the country was facing, with unemployment rising and the loss of confidence in the Government. There was a series of attacks against the Pistols and people involved with them, with special attention paid to Johnny Rotten. He suffered two assaults in three days, one of which left him with severed tendons in one hand and a machete wound in the leg which would have been serious had he not been wearing thick leather trousers. The attacks were a signal for a summer-long spate of violence between Teds and Punks reminiscent of those of Mods and Rockers in the 1960s. The Pistols were forced to lie low; Vicious and Rotten rang Glitterbest to say that they should leave the country. A tour of Scandinavia was quickly arranged.

Before they left, 'Pretty Vacant' was rush released on 2 July 1977 to capitalise on the Pistols' exposure. It was a 'safe' release and did not suffer from the bans of the previous singles; it would reach number 6 in the charts, behind the number 1 sounds of Kenny Rogers' 'Lucille'. The next week Nancy Spungen appeared in court charged with carrying a 'protective' truncheon in her handbag. She avoided being sent back to America by Sid's declaring his intent to marry her. Her deportation would have pleased many of the people around Sid Vicious, who was heavily involved with heroin by now. He and Nancy fought a lot, and were only quiet when they were stoned.

The Sex Pistols travelled to Copenhagen on 13 June for the start of the tour. While they were away, their promotional video of 'Pretty Vacant' was shown on *Top of the Pops*, and the band appeared on the programme on their return. The two-week tour was a success, and the band was more relaxed than it had ever been. Sid was not taking any hard drugs for the duration, and his live playing was much more acceptable than the standard which was necessary in the studio; for recording tracks towards the planned album the Pistols had had to

Sid with 'Gimme a Fix' smeared on his chest

The final gig at Winterland, San Francisco

bring back Glen Matlock as a session player.

On their return from Sweden, the Pistols were involved in arguments over the proposed film which McLaren had been trying to get off the ground. He would pour £50,000 into pre-production for a history of the Sex Pistols called *Who Killed Bambi*, to be directed by *Beyond the Valley of the Dolls'* Russ Meyer. Although Steve Jones and Paul Cook were happy about the idea, Rotten and Vicious were adamant in their rejection of it. 'I hate films', said Sid, 'because people have to ... play people that they're not'.

Trying to continue the live exposure, the band set about an undercover tour of

England, called the SPOTS tour (Sex Pistols on tour secretly). They had several names, from 'special guests' to the Tax Exiles, Acne Rabble and the Hamsters, and would drop out of a gig if word got out beforehand. This took them into September, during which time Sid took a flat in Maida Vale with a seven-year lease on it, about which Malcolm McLaren was heard to say 'that's OK. He'll be dead by then'. Sid returned to Nancy and his drug habit, while the budget for *Who Killed Bambi* soared, and the album *Never Mind the Bollocks* (a title provided by Steve Jones) was coming together. As a stopgap, 'Holidays in the Sun' was released on 15 October, in a sleeve which had to be pulled because of a copyright complaint by the Belgian Tourist Service. In the same week the film collapsed when its finances fell through and Russ Meyer walked away from it. However, *Never Mind the Bollocks* was successfully released on the 28th of the month, to 'four letter word' headlines and bans from the major retailers. They didn't stop it entering the charts at number 1, knocking Cliff Richard's *40 Golden Greats* off the top. This was the last recording the band as a whole would make.

The title of the album was the subject of censorship by the music press, and the police brought an action against one record shop for displaying the cover in its window. The case was lost, to the reluctance of the chairman of the bench, by the proving of the historical meaning of the word 'bollocks' as 'nonsense'. The media expressed its disgust at the outcome, bringing the reply from Johnny Rotten, 'bollocks'.

In the meantime, Sid Vicious was keeping his profile in the press, with the smashing-up of a hotel room, and reports of his and Nancy's arrest on a 'drugs probe', for which no charges were brought pending examination of substances. McLaren and the other Pistols attempted to bribe Nancy to go back to America, shoving her into a cab with a plane ticket and money, but she wouldn't go. They managed to ban her from most of the gigs, but every time she managed to find Sid, he was back on the drugs again. Rotten tried to get Sid off the habit several times,

Sid Vicious is arrested for Nancy's murder

Chloe Webb and Gary Oldman in the film
Sid and Nancy

locking him in his room and putting up
with the noise and abuse of Sid's coming
down, but it was a no-win situation, and
each time, Sid chose to return to the
dark side of his nature. The Pistols took a
short tour of Holland in December, and
the party would have to take it in turns
staying up all night with Sid, to keep
him away from dealers. He was starting
to lose himself on stage, which antag-
onised Jones and Cook, who had always
been the most serious band members.

The Dutch trip was the first leg on a
proposed extended jaunt, which would
take in America and Europe, with pre-
liminary dates in England under their
own name. Half of the eight English gigs
were cancelled, and the year ended in
frustration over visas for America

because of their various criminal re-cords. Only when their new American label, Warners, agreed to pay a surety of $1 million were the visas granted, and the delay meant that only the southern half of the country could be covered.

The year had been one of acceleration within the independent music arena. The number of bands, the small retail outlets, the fanzine industry, had grown with the Sex Pistols, but the original unity of the punk movement had been split by both internal and external pressures. The opposition that the Pistols had set up meant that Punk had now all but run its course; the energy which had fed the initial movement was found to be something either to move on from, or collapse under, and the New Wave of hard, but more mainstream groups would be the way forward. The *Record Mirror* Readers' Poll for 1977 put the Sex Pistols fourth in the Best Band category (first was T Rex), and top of the Bore of the Year spot. The top three New Bands were the Boomtown Rats, Tom Robinson and the Stranglers.

Taking Civilization To The Barbarians

On 3 January 1978 the Sex Pistols flew to New York on a two-week visa, where they were taken in tow by Warner representatives determined to keep the $1 million bond safe. *Never Mind the Bollocks* had been released in the States to prime the country for Britain's Punk Royal Family, and an antidote to the Bee Gees' *Saturday Night Fever* – the start of the disco fever which would sweep the nation that year. *Never Mind the Bollocks* bubbled around the bottom of the Billboard top hundred album charts; it would take until 1987 for it to attain gold disc status, the same year that it would be *Rolling Stone*'s second greatest rock album of all time.

The Pistols caught an onward flight for the first gig at Atlanta, which they bombed. Sid disappeared after the concert to find drugs and suffered the first of several beatings from the security staff, who took their job seriously. The second night he gashed himself with a knife, and the combined security and press divisions tried not to let him out of their sight from then on. By the second gig at San Antonio, neither Rotten or Vicious were on speaking terms with

Malcolm McLaren, and the show was a model of aggressive rock'n'roll, from both the bottle throwing crowd and the frustrated Pistols. Sid roused the audience by calling them a 'bunch of f****** faggots', clubbing a dissenter with his bass and temporarily stopping the show. A full beer can in the face was not enough to prevent his taunts.

He considered by now that his status allowed him a free rein, and wanted to 'be like Iggy Pop and die before I'm thirty', though it was pointed out to him that Iggy was over thirty and still alive. Jones and Cook refused to travel on the coach any more and from then on flew to each destination. Rotten and Vicious remained on the coach, trying to evade their minders at every opportunity.

On one stop they managed to slip into a diner, where Sid was recognised and challenged by a local, who stubbed a cigarette out on his hand. In reply, Sid cut his hand as he was eating and let the blood drip onto his steak as he continued his meal. At the next concert he appeared with magic marker highlighting the scars on his chest which formed the words 'gimme a fix', and played with three out of four of his bass strings broken; 'a living circus', Rotten declared. By the time the Sex Pistols reached San Francisco for the 14 January show they had been banned from several hotel chains, and refused work permits for the next stage of the tour in Finland.

McLaren had the idea of filling the five-day space that the Finnish ban caused

with a trip to Rio de Janeiro for a
meeting with train robber Ronnie
Biggs. This would be after the gig at
Winterland, the biggest the Pistols had
played, with a capacity of 5,000 and a
high stage like that of the star gigs that
they had always derided. It was a disaster;
the sound was terrible, they played
badly, but even worse in the eyes of
the Pistols, the crowd did not seem to
mind a display against which they should
have rioted.

Two days later, the Sex Pistols im-
ploded. Rotten decided that he had
had enough, and after talking with
Jones and Cook, who had both decided
to quit, he had a final confrontation with
McLaren at the hotel, after which he was
no longer in the band. Sid Vicious called

Rotten with a garbled message to the effect that he too was finished with the Pistols, and a few hours after took an overdose. He was taken to a doctor who prescribed methadone pills, which got him on a flight to New York. However, the valium that he took on top of the methadone caused him to slip into a coma, and he was admitted to hospital on arrival at the airport. Jones and Cook took the flight to Rio, Rotten hung around in New York for a few days, and the British press was full of the death throes of the band that had ended at its own logical conclusion.

The next few months saw a rapid increase in the fragmentation of what had begun with Punk, as the Pistols' break-up lost the movement its last

excuse for unity. Bands broke away
into New Wave, Ted, Mod, Power
Pop and Glam factions, with only the
banner of Rock Against Racism to hold
them together. As far as the members of
the Pistols were concerned, Malcolm
McLaren continued his attempts to get
a film off the ground, John Lydon (he
reclaimed his real surname) formed
Public Image Ltd and set about taking
Glitterbest to court, while Steve Jones
and Paul Cook continued recording for
themselves.

Sid and Nancy returned to their drug-
based existence; they were filmed with
Sid burning Nancy with a cigarette and
playing with a hunting knife. He was
persuaded to go to Paris, where he
recorded 'My Way' in an inspired piece

of symbol-knocking. The song was
released in June on a double-A single
with the Jones/Cook/Biggs song 'No
One is Innocent – A Punk Prayer', and
reached number 6 in the charts mainly
due to the Frank Sinatra pastiche. Sid
was also roused from his inactivity to
record versions of the Eddie Cochran
songs 'C'mon Everybody' and 'Something Else'. The other times he appeared
in public he would inevitably get into
fights, and he and Nancy became ad-
dicted to the methadone which they had
decided to take in an attempt to get off
heroin. At the end of August he played a
'Sid Sods Off' gig at Camden's Electric
Ballroom, before moving to New York.

Who Killed Bambi?

In New York, Sid and Nancy took room 100 at the Chelsea Hotel on West 23rd Street, a run-down artists' base, but their hopes of a fresh start were soon dashed by continued drug use, constant violence and the town's refusal to accept them as the stars which they proclaimed themselves to be. There was a concert in September 1978, with the remnants of the New York Dolls and the Clash's Mick Jones backing Sid, but by October, their bad general health and worsening arguments were isolating them in the same way that had happened in London.

In the early morning of 12 October, Sid woke from a drug-induced sleep to find Nancy in a pool of blood under the bathroom sink, with his hunting knife in her side. The police arrived, he admitted to killing her and was charged with second degree murder. Although several rival stories would be thrown into the pot, involving drug-dealers, burglars and a suicide pact, the actual details as described by Sid are that earlier that night, while waiting for drugs to be delivered, he went around banging on other doors in the hotel. He was hit on the nose by the night attendant, and when he went back to the room, Nancy hit him again on the same spot. He pulled the knife on her, and the play-acting which they had performed so often became real, as they both pushed forward at the same time.

Sid's initial confusion turned to despair, as he realised that he was alone, and told reporters how distraught he was at losing her. 'Nancy was great because she and I were the same', he said, 'we both hated everyone'. British reaction to the stabbing was generally one of 'it was only a question of time'. Vivienne Westwood brought out a deliberately provocative T-shirt with the slogan 'She's dead, I'm alive, I'm yours'. Nine days after a court hearing of 13 October allowed bail of

$50,00 (put up by Virgin), Sid tried to commit suicide. His mother had flown out to be with him, and it was she who phoned Malcolm McLaren, who had flown out as soon as he heard of Sid's arrest, to beg him to come round to their hotel. He had, however, cut his arm, rather than his wrists, and McLaren rang for an ambulance, though Sid asked him to get him some heroin so that he could finish the job and be with Nancy. He was taken to the psychiatric ward at Bellevue Hospital but discharged after a few days, and reentered New York life with a new girl, Michelle Robinson.

Sid's bail was confirmed at a hearing on 21 November, although he was described as someone who 'cultivates an

image of antagonism and has a flagrant
disregard for constitutional authority'.
He proved the statement less than three
weeks later at a nightclub, when he
attacked Patti Smith's brother, Todd,
with a broken bottle, after assaulting
Todd's girlfriend. He was taken to
prison at Riker's Island, where it was
decided he should stay until a court
appearance on 1 February 1979. The
enforced period without drugs meant
that by that date Sid was drug-free.
Malcolm McLaren planned to meet
him the following day, when he was
expected to be released, to take him to
Miami to do an album which would
pay for the coming murder trial. However, the judge let Sid out on the day of
the hearing, so Sid went back to
Michelle Robinson's flat with his

mother and a few friends and took some heroin.

After a meal some more heroin was brought in; this supply was purer than usual, and the combined effect of that and Sid's detoxification caused him to collapse on the bed. He came round, however, and was left to sleep it off. But sometime during the night, he woke up, found the stash and took another hit. The next morning he was discovered to be dead; he had taken more than his jump-started body could bear.

Sid Vicious' textbook rock death had begun his path to icon status, a path which started with the rumour that the urn containing his ashes had been dropped and smashed at Heathrow airport, and led to the 1986 Alex Cox film, *Sid and Nancy*. The release of 'Something Else' took place less than three weeks after his death and got him to number three in the charts, as would 'C'mon Everybody'. Sid's three singles were also featured on the soundtrack to the film which Malcolm McLaren had struggled to bring out for so long, *The Great Rock'n'Roll Swindle*, and collected for a twelve inch EP called 'Sid Sings', whose sleeve featured a Sid Vicious Action Man doll lying in a coffin. The 'Action Man' image conveys the double-edged truth in the myth of Sid Vicious; the toy soldier behind the street-fighter. He was a malleable person, and could have been directed in many different ways, but once he had taken on his persona, there were few people around him who saw a happy ending for him. As Sid's earlier hero, David Bowie, had sung in 'Ziggy Stardust', 'He took it all too far'.